Tendering My Resignation;

a true story

Jessica Lincoln

Revolution

A Division of Inkletting Press

Seattle

Print ISBN - 13: 978-1-950295-02-9

Ebook ISBN-13: 978-1-950295-03-6

I have no medical training except the CPR class I took five years ago in high school. I'm no expert on cancer, or the cervix. So why am I here? Moral support. Nothing more. I'm an innocent bystander... to my best friend's pap smear.

Dr. Cardosa's head pops up from behind the sheet draped across Adrian's mid-section.

"Adrian, your cervix is healing nicely," she announces in her faint Brazilian accent. Then she turns to me.

"Do you want to see it?"

"What." I glance at Adrian and her face mirrors the equal parts shock and horror I feel.

"Do you want to see it?" Dr. Cardosa asks again.

There's no protocol in my arsenal for a situation like this. Is it rude to say no? I glance over at Adrian in a silent "what now?" But she just shrugs her shoulders in equal disbelief. Despite every cell in my body screaming no, I hesitantly move myself into position beside the doctor.

"There it is, that's the cervix," Dr. Cardosa says, spreading Adrian's legs farther apart and pointing with her pen and then grabbing my shoulders to move me into a better position. Looking between another woman's legs may be just another day at the office for Dr. Cardosa, but for me, this is a first; a first I certainly don't need front row seating to.

"Actually Addie," I say, partly in wonder, but more in a desperate attempt to make the situation even a little less awkward, "it really is amazing. Really."

"Really?" she asks me. And it really is…not the cervix part so much as that's where they performed laser surgery less than a month ago to remove cancer from her cervix – for the second time. Well, that and not getting her bikini area waxed, even during the winter, seems contradictory to all of Adrian's OCD tendencies.

"No Addie, really. I wish you could see this," I tell her, hoping I sound convincing.

"Oh! Here you go!" Dr. Cardosa chimes in, whipping out a mirror from God knows where. "You want to see?" she asks, offering Adrian the mirror.

***

Despite Adrian's protests, Dr. Cardosa immediately admits her to the ER for intravenous fluids and tests regarding her unexplainable 30-pound weight loss. Whatever "freshman fifteen" Adrian may have been carrying is long gone. The Adrian I see when I look at her now holds only a slight resemblance to what I saw at Christmas a month ago. The doctors take Adrian to the back to X-ray her stomach and I'm directed to the waiting room.

When I walk in, I instantly gravitate towards the chair presenting the least probability of contact with anyone else. The walls crawl from the florescent lighting, the incessant buzzing becoming a mosquito trapped in my ear canal. The carpet, a turquoise-maroon-green-gold confusing mass has seen better days. My eyes follow the pattern around the room, ending back at my feet. Before me sits a stain that can only be vomit. No wonder this spot was wide open. I pick up my purse and backpack and move to a different seat. In an effort to divert my attention from any more potential body fluid stains, I begin focusing on the people around me.

A man I purposely avoided sits in the far corner. I'm not sure if it's his age, his hygiene, or his incessant rocking back and forth that makes me cower from him, but everything about him screams "unclean." Under the haze of the florescent lights I envision an aura of disease radiating from him. He coughs a thick, rasping, hacking, cough into his hand. Clearly the cough was productive because he then wipes his hand on the adjoining chair.

Mental note: don't sit in that one.

I sigh.

If there isn't some kind of airline clause for a crappy vacation, there should be. I feel strangely guilty spending my vacation like this. Adrian's mom paid to fly me out as her birthday present, I feel like fun is mandatory. We should be shopping or at the beach; not in the ER. The last minute gynecologist appointment was merely supposed to be a detour, not a road block. Of course I want to be here for Adrian, but I feel like it should be on my dime, not her mom's.

Across from me sits a Hispanic woman and her two children. The woman is abnormally small, about five foot and barely 90 pounds. Her children, a little girl approximately two years old and a boy, maybe five are squirmish and antsy. A stocky blonde with her hair slicked back into a tight bun sits next to the woman, helping to keep the little girl under control. She bounces her in her lap, keeping a tight grip on her, never once smiling at her or making the seemingly instinctual surprise faces that we all seem to revert to with children. Although she is realistically only a couple inches taller than the first woman, she exudes the authority of a six-foot-200-pound male. Yet in her Channel knock-off business suit, high heels and briefcase, she is still a lady. She looks like a Helga; sturdy and stern.

She readjusts the little girl on her lap and suddenly they have my full attention. The shift in the woman's position exposed the medical bracelet attached to the little girl's wrist. I notice a similar medical bracelet around the little boy's arm. I search for one on their mother but there's none. I had simply assumed these children were waiting for someone, never stopping to consider the possibility they could be patients. What purpose could they possibly have in this hospital?

The little girl lets out a slight whine and begins to squirm from the blond woman's lap. As she slides herself off, her stained little pink and white striped shirt catches on Helga's knees, sliding up past the little girl's round belly and exposes what appears to be a scar approximately 1 inch in diameter and 3 inches in length. My stomach lurches and I just about leave my own body fluid stain on the carpet.

"It could just be a birthmark," I tell myself, wishing I wore contacts. I'm not about to pull out my glasses to gawk at this little girl's stomach.

A door opens and in steps a busty blonde policewoman with her short hair pulled tightly into a low ponytail. The hug of her uniform on her hips and the ample protrusion of her chest makes her look like a stripper or singing telegram. She walks straight to the little boy and kneels beside him, gently clasping his wrist, turning it over as if inspecting it. She continues to kneel next to him, speaking gently, his little head nodding in agreement. She rises, and with one hand on the little boys back, gently guides him, his mother, sister, and the stocky blonde I now assume to be their social worker, back into the door from which she came.

An older male nurse grabs my attention and motions for me to follow him. He leads me back to Adrian's curtained portion of the ER. I pull up the doctor's stool to sit beside her while we wait for the test results. A couple minutes later, in walks a tan, six foot tall guy dressed in a hoodie, surf shorts and Vans. Adrian's ex-boyfriend, Dan. Knowing Adrian, this is the first and last time we'll meet. He's one of the many while I remain the constant.

"Hey babe," he says, bending down to kiss Adrian on the forehead. "Happy birthday," he hands her a clumsily wrapped package.

"What is it?" she asks, unwrapping the gift, even though it's obviously a book. "Oh, it's the one I wanted," she says, smiling up at him.

A female nurse comes in and begins fussing with some charts and Adrian's IV.

"Um, excuse me," Adrian says, reaching towards the plastic bag hanging from the side of her bed. "This thing is getting heavy."

The nurse turns and gives her a condescending look. "That's because it's filled with urine," she says and walks away.

Adrian falls back against her pillow, "I hate the ER."

"Do they know what's wrong with you yet?" Dan asks.

"I don't know, they're saying maybe there's something wrong with my colon."

Adrian chatters on about her colon while I sit on the edge of my stool, waiting for the opportunity to jump in. When Adrian starts in on the possibility of a colonoscopy, Dan casually picks up the book he's given to her and begins to thumb through it. I have my chance.

"Addie," I lean in and whisper as quietly as I can, "do you know your colon is basically your butthole?"

Her eyes widen and she shoots upright. "Oh Jesus. Are you kidding me?"

I shake my head.

"Damn it. I *hate* the ER."

***

Dan leaves soon after the awkward silence that follows Adrian's extensive report on the state of her colon, and shortly afterwards a doctor comes in to tell us he'd like to admit Adrian overnight for observation.

"But it's my birthday," she says.

"Well, I don't know what to say to that."

"But I can't spend my birthday in the hospital." Adrian looks at me and we both silently add a single word to the end of her sentence: Again.

"We haven't figured out what's wrong with you yet and with your medical history, thirty pounds is a lot to lose in a month. You're severely dehydrated and…"

Neither one of us is listening. We both know there's no way Adrian's spending her birthday in the hospital.

"But it's my choice, right?" she says. "I mean, you can't make me stay, right?"

"Well, no. I can't make you stay, but if you care about your health, I strongly advise you to stay here, continue to receive fluids, and let us do our job."

"Um, okay. Tomorrow." Adrian moves to get up and realizes she's still tethered to the bed by her catheter.

"Okay, okay," the doctor puts his hands on her shoulders, pushing her back towards her pillow. "It's going to take a couple minutes to get someone here to take the catheter out, so in the meantime, at least let me give you one more bag of potassium. Deal?"

"Deal."

"And, you come back here first thing in the morning."

"Deal." Adrian nods her head solemnly.

He then turns to me. "If anything happens, you get her straight back here. She's your responsibility."

I nod my head too, immediately feeling the weight he's just placed on me.

"And happy…" he looks down at his chart and then turns to Adrian, "twenty-fourth birthday!"

"Thanks," Adrian says with a death-glare.

***

T he admitting room of Tampa's hospital is a vast improvement over that of the ER. The glass windows and doors surrounding us help diffuse the effects of the florescent lighting, and the smell of flowers from the gift shop waft throughout the room. I can't decide if the flowers give the room added life or the aura of a funeral parlor, but their perfume is a welcome disguise to the underlying smell of sickness hanging in the air.

Adrian looks significantly worse this morning. Looking at her you would never know we spent a mellow night eating spaghetti and relaxing with her friends. Her eyes droop from exhaustion and the bags beneath them practically have her eyes swollen shut.

Adrian asks me for her book and I reach into her backpack and pull out <u>The Tibetan Book of Living and Dying</u>.

"Nice." I tell her sarcastically.

I open a page at random and read the passage aloud:

Impermanence

There is no place on earth where death cannot find us... If there were any way of sheltering from death's blows – I am not the man to recoil from it... But it is madness to think that you can succeed...

To begin depriving death of its greatest advantage over us, let us adopt a way clean contrary to that common one; let us deprive death of its strangeness, let us frequent it, let us get used to it; let us have nothing more often in mind than death...We do not know where death awaits us: so let us wait for it everywhere. To practice death is to practice freedom. A man who has

learned how to die has un-
learned how to be a slave.

-Montaigne-

We begin talking about death, what it means, where we go... I from the point of the living and Adrian, not quite from the point of the dying, but no longer from the perspective of the living. She talks like she's straddling two worlds, not sure which one she belongs to and with no choice in the matter – like she's passively standing on the sidelines in PE waiting to be chosen for a team.

I begin reflecting on my own recent struggle in defining who, if anything, God is. Do I believe? I've been told I should and I'm scared to not, but my doubts are inescapable. The thought of death being the end-all of existence scares me. My innate human drive towards survival refuses to allow me to believe death is the end. But I still cannot, as of yet, embrace what I don't know. Yes, I feel the world beyond the material existence of my life as it is now. I feel the energy and movement of the universe all around me. There *is* something greater than just me. But whether it's God or simply gravity, I just don't know. But I've chosen to believe. It's a conscious choice. Faith is what I suppose the optimistic would call it. The definition of self-delusion by anyone else's standards.

When it's Adrian's turn, she looks to me wide-eyed and scared.

"I don't believe in God. I think when we die, that's it. It's over. There's no spirit, no ghosts. I don't believe any of it."

"So what happens when we die then?"

"We die. We decay. The end."

"But I don't want it to be the end," I tell her, like she has power over any of it.

"I don't either, but that doesn't change anything. I can't believe in something just because I want it to be true. I'd be lying to myself. That's one thing cancer teaches you. You can lie to other people, but you can't lie to yourself. No matter how hard you pretend, deep down, you still know you're nothing but a liar."

"Adrian?"

"Yeah."

"Why haven't you told your friends here?"

"No one wants to be friends with that girl."

"What girl?"

"The girl who's going to die."

"But you're not going to die."

"Whatever. People don't want to be around sick people."

"I think your friends may surprise you."

"Do you know what happened when Dan told his parents I had cervical cancer?"

"What."

"They looked at me like I was a leper. You don't understand. Cervical cancer's different."

"What do you mean?"

"I don't have warts."

"What?"

"I don't have genital warts. But I still have cervical cancer. There's this stigma attached to cervical cancer. People just assume you're a slut and you have genital warts and you did something to cause your cancer."

"Addie, I don't think –"

"It's like lung cancer. People assume you're a smoker and you deserve it. Besides, I don't exactly want everyone discussing my vagina."

I can understand that. Why is it that cancer seems to be attracted to the embarrassing parts; the parts we're not supposed to talk about? There's no finger cancer movement like breast cancer. There's no elbow cancer awareness month like colon cancer. Or what about prostate cancer? It's usually completely inappropriate to discuss

penis parts, but the second it involves cancer, it's suddenly accepta-
ble dinner conversation. Colon cancer, breast cancer, cervical cancer,
testicular cancer; all nice names for cancer of the asshole, boobs,
vagina plug and balls.

***

Finally, a young professionally dressed Hispanic woman ap-
proaches us and instructs us to follow her. Moving at a brisk
pace she disappears into an office towards the back – Jackie
Joyner in high-heels. Realizing we aren't moving as efficiently as
she is, she reappears in the doorway of the office. She stands there,
one hand on the doorknob, the other extended towards us as if gal-
lantly holding the door.

I feel myself beginning to dislike her as she stands there, watching as I awkwardly struggle towards her; weighted down by my lap-
top, backpack, and purse hanging from one shoulder and Adrian's
backpack and overnight bag hanging from the other. The bags slide
from my shoulders to my forearms as I attempt to help Adrian, who
has yet to figure out the precise left/right hand combination to agilely
maneuver her wheelchair through the maze that makes up the waiting room.

When we're finally situated at the desk, the admitting process
begins. Insurance company information – well don't they have it in
the computer? Oh, wait, no, it's in Adrian's backpack, we did re-
member it… Who is Adrian's official admitting doctor – well he was
supposed to have called ahead to make all the arrangements… What
is her purpose – well she did have cervical cancer but we don't know
if that's it… But she's being admitted by a gastroenterologist, not a
gynecologist? – well, okay then I guess she's technically being admitted for weight loss… Why? – from severe diarrhea if you must
get personal…

She quickly inputs Adrian's information into the computer, her
long, blatantly fake magenta nails click-clacking on the keyboard.

"Sign here," she thrusts a clipboard towards Adrian and in one fluid motion, points to the bottom with the pen she offers.

Adrian places the clipboard on her lap and looks down as she slowly and purposefully positions the pen in her hand, allowing it to hover at the bottom of the page where the woman had indicated.

"Uh-oh," I think to myself, *"this woman isn't going to even know what hit her."*

Adrian has perfected this evil eye that can evoke a confession from a Navy Seal. To the untrained individual this look can be a shattering blow. It's just the precise combination of *"Are you an idiot?"* *"Do you think I'm an idiot?"* *"Don't lie to me I'll kill you,"* and *"By the way, I already know the answer I'm simply allowing you to set your own trap."* It really can be nerve-racking. I know Adrian gives me the look at times, even without reason... perhaps practicing, perhaps simply playing with my mind, perhaps even becoming drunk off her own power.

I watch as Adrian executes this perfectly bitchy slow-motion blink. Her head is angled downward. As her eyes slowly open, in one slow, drawn-out motion, she begins raising her gaze. Her head slowly follows until she has eye contact with the woman, leveling her head and staring the woman down head-on. Her gaze lingers, her face remaining blank and void of emotion. Adrian is obviously enjoying every second of this. She is completely comfortable in this woman's discomfort.

Without breaking eye contact, Adrian's hand, still hovering at the bottom as if taunting the woman, slowly, purposefully, moves up to the top of the paper. She looks down and scribbles her initials at the top in a fury. Through lowered gaze she meets the woman's eyes once again. I contemplate feeling sorry for this woman. I've been the victim of this look before; it's absolutely menacing. Adrian's eyes remain fixed on her just long enough to shoot a couple hate-filled daggers towards her while her hand slowly drifts to the bottom of the page. Adrian's eyes flash downward briefly, just long enough for her to get her bearings and then she once again locks her eyes upon the woman, gaze fixed, as she scribbles her signature.

Never once breaking her stare, she places the clipboard calmly on the desk and slides it over to the woman, allowing her hand to rest there and her gaze to linger just a bit longer than comfortable. The woman begins to fidget, shifting in her chair, trying to ignore the fact that Adrian is still staring at her. Avoiding eye contact, she stands and assures us someone will be with us shortly to take Adrian to her room, and then hurries out in the same efficient manner she ushered us in with. Adrian has broken this woman without saying a word. It's the classiest fuck-you I've ever seen.

"Yeah, you know why you're a bitch," Adrian says once the woman is safely out of earshot.

Not understanding a thing about the scene that just transpired before me, I turn to Adrian with a confused look.

"Read it," she says, handing me the form.

I read it.

"So?"

"Read it again."

I read it again.

I still don't understand so I read it yet again… a light comes on.

The woman never mentioned to Adrian that by *not* initialing the top of the form she was waving her rights to sue for "any dispute as to medical malpractice… whether any medical services rendered… were unnecessary or unauthorized or were improperly, negligently, or incorrectly rendered… "

I can't believe it; consent by omission. But I guess that's how even our elections work…

"Do you know what any lawyer would have told me if I tried to dispute that?"

We exchange a knowing look and almost in unison; "You should have read it before you signed it."

*****

After what seems like days, but is only a couple hours later, we're finally led upstairs to the fifth floor; Adrian's new home for an undetermined amount of time. A wave of relief washes over me when I realize we'll be the only occupants of this room.

We wait. And wait. And wait…

We pass the time arranging Adrian's room, Adrian directing me from her spot on the bed as I carefully arrange our toiletries in a neat line along the counter by her sink. I take careful pains to make sure everything is within her reach from her bed which runs from one end of the counter to the other. I pull back the hideous pastel rainbow curtains to allow the sun passage into the starkness of her room. I hang her clothes in her closet and place her shoes by the foot of the bed. I look to the corner by the closet and notice a sign:

"Although minutes may seem like hours, please be patient."

I laugh.

After we're situated…for about an hour, a nurse finally comes to take Adrian's information…

"Hiii, yhoo A-dee-anne?" asks a young Asian nurse dressed in blue scrubs with the nametag "June."

"Oh shit," I think as I look over, watching Adrian's jaw tighten. Now, Adrian's defiantly not prejudice, but she *is* impatient.

"Whaah yhoo sim-nons?"

Adrian looks at me in panic as I begin to mouth "symptoms."

"Yhoo poooohh?" June asks.

"Yes, she's had pretty bad diarrhea lately," I answer, barely stifling a giggle.

"Du yhoo hawv hnie sycooloogoocoo pwobwems?"

"I can't understand what you're saying," Adrian tells her flatly, obviously frustrated.

"Do you have any psychological problems," I translate. "You know, fear of hospitals, fear of needles, are you a hypochondriac…"

17

June nods in agreement, injecting little "yaw's" and "aha's" for punctuation.

I try to give June a look that tells her she's not helping, but she doesn't get the message.

"You mean other than the fact that I'm sick, I'm scared, and I'm sitting in a hospital bed without my mother?" Adrian retorts. "No."

I try explaining to June that no, Adrian doesn't have a problem being here,

she knows why she's here, she wants to be here because she wants to get better, but she might need a little extra nurturing. I know the angle Adrian's going for – some extra blankets, maybe an extra dessert or two, if someone leaves without their flowers, well, Adrian just loves flowers…But June just doesn't get it. Adrian sits in her bed, her thoughts written clearly across her face. She is willing June to drop dead on the spot. I get it. I get frustrated enough when I have to deal with an accent this thick at the drive thru, but in a hospital, it's down right scary.

I strain my neck over June's shoulder and watch as she checks the "IN DENIAL" box on Adrian's form. It's all I can do to not rip the pen from her hand and start filling it out myself.

As June leaves, Adrian falls back against her pillows with an exaggerated sigh.

"This is going to be a long one," I think to myself.

The rest of my day is spent trying to conquer the language barrier with June while Adrian is poked and prodded from all angles; X-rays, CT scan, catheter, ultrasound, blood work, stool samples… Doctors come and go, consulting June's chart and finding new mistakes at every turn. I'm suddenly thankful Adrian knew enough to sign her initials earlier. If there's any instance in which a leg may be unduly amputated, June's lack of command for the English language lays the perfect foundation.

The following day a different nurse enters, this time a cheery male. He pulls me aside.

"Well, I think maybe we know the cause of her sickness," he

whispers to me as if Adrian were a child unable to participate in her own health care. "She has cancer," he tells me in a voice so low I feel myself straining to hear.

"Where?" I ask.

He points to the words "cervical cancer" written in the "diagnosis" section of her chart.

"Has it spread?" I ask.

He gives me a confused look.

"She already knows she has cancer," I tell him. "She just had surgery for it a month ago."

"Oh," he says as if dumbfounded. "I'll be right back."

I already know exactly where this is going.

He steps back in the room, the apology written across his face and the relief evident in his voice, "Her history was written down in the diagnosis section of her chart."

June.

This is so much worse than the drive thru.

***

After twenty-four hours in the hospital, I figure it's time to call Adrian's mom. I walk down the hallway to have some privacy and take a deep breath to prepare myself for the conversation I'm about to have. It's not every day I tell a mother her daughter's in the hospital. Again.

"What?" She sighs. "What for?"

"They're not sure yet. She's lost about thirty pounds since Christmas so they're trying to figure out why."

Another sigh on the end of the phone.

"Well make sure they have the right insurance information and the bill gets sent straight to me."

"Um, okay. Are you coming down here?"

"Honey, my schedule's really packed for the next couple of days. Can you just handle it from your end and keep me posted?"

"Um, okay." I shouldn't be surprised. Adrian and I have been best friends for ten years. I've had plenty of time to accept her mom's parenting style. But coming from a mother who traveled 1300 miles when my dog had surgery, I don't think I'll ever get used to it. "I have to be back at school in a couple of days though," I say, feeling like I'm letting her mom down. Playing the role of Adrian's emotional mother is a job I've had for a while.

Another sigh.

"Okay, when do you leave?"

"Sunday."

"Alright. I'll see what I can do."

I hang up with Adrian's mom, shocked at the responsibility she's left me with. She's asked me to do her job – to nurture Adrian, to comfort her, to asses what's going on with her and to make decisions about her health – she's asked me to be the mother of a sick child. That's a lot more than what I thought I'd be doing here. It's not a burden. I want to be a part of this with Adrian, but I don't feel like I'm old enough to do this. The state says I am, but what do they know?

Walking back towards Adrian's room, I can hear her arguing with June from down the hallway by the nurses' station.

"I'm fine! I don't need help! No, I don't need you to come in with me!"

I quickly turn the corner in time to watch Adrian try to shake June off with her good arm. June reaches for her again, but this time goes for the arm with the IV needle in it.

"Ahhhhhhh!" Adrian lets out an overly dramatic wail and I launch myself between the two of them.

"I've got it! I've got it!" I yell, as Adrian grabs the bar of her IV stand and rips it away from June and then marches towards her private bathroom.

"Sheeee fooooool?" June says in her own defense, pointing to Adrian.

Adrian's head whips around, eyes narrowed, "Did she just call me a fool?"

"Fall. She's worried you're going to fall," I tell Adrian as I shove June out the door and shut it firmly.

"Oh for God's sakes. I'm going to be sitting down. Where am I supposed to fall from?" Adrian yells after her.

"Adrian!" I use my best authoritative voice.

"God, it's bad enough having to talk about my shits with every person who walks through the door, but now I can't even do it in privacy?" she says from the bathroom, with the door wide open. "What did my mom say?"

"Um, she said she loves you?" I call back from over by the door.

"What? I can't hear you. Come here," Adrian commands from her porcelain throne.

"Addie, she's not coming," I decide to give it to her straight. It's a blow that can't really be softened. "Maybe in a couple of days, but not right now."

"You did tell her I'm in the hospital."

"Yeah, Aids, I did."

Adrian's jaw tightens. "Let's go," she says, marching out of the bathroom, IV stand in tow. She fishes through her purse and, satisfied with its contents, throws it at me. "Come on."

We casually walk past the nurses' station, but it's impossible to be discreet while dragging an electronic IV stand. A nurse immediately rushes towards us – not June, she's in the far corner of the station, cowering from the wrath of Adrian.

"What do you need dear?" she asks, reaching to give Adrian a hand.

"Um, I just want to go for a little walk, if that's okay," Adrian tells her meekly, all traces of the devil patient vanished.

"Oh, of course hon. Do you want a wheelchair?"

"No, I want to walk," she says with a soft smile.

"Okay." The nurse says, turning back around. June looks like even more of a fool now than she did before.

Adrian shuffles down the hall, her boxers and bare back exposed through the slit up the back of her hospital gown every couple of steps.

We turn the corner, out of view of the nurses' station and she looks back over her shoulder and down both hallways before pushing the elevator button. When the bell dings she shoves her IV stand in and impatiently pushes the button to the ground floor.

We wander about the first floor, looking for the most discreet exit possible. We find one on the other side of the building, down a back hallway. The doors slide open and we both step out into the warm Florida breeze. I had almost forgot I was in Tampa. The stale air of the hospital makes it easy to forget the world outside its cement walls.

"Hurry!" Adrian motions for her purse. She digs through and finds her cigarettes and then looks around both ways, taking a moment to smirk at the "No Smoking" sign above her head, before lighting up. She wheels her IV over to the curb and sits down, but her IV cord is too short for her to comfortably rest her hand by her side. So she sits on the curb, arm propped up, and smokes her cigarette. I join her on the curb and light my own cigarette, stretching out my legs and leaning back to enjoy myself.

"Are you almost ready?" she says before I'm even able to exhale.

"Huh?" I look to Adrian's hand and it's holding not much more than the butt of her cigarette. She takes one more long drag and quickly exhales and throws her butt down on the ground. "Did you even enjoy that?"

"It's not about the enjoyment. It's about the nicotine. Let's go," she says, waving her arm at me.

"Just give me a second. If I'm going to kill myself, I'm going to enjoy it."

"Fine. But I'm going to wait inside. I don't want them catching me out here."

"'Kay," I say, turning to watch her go.

She drags her IV stand towards the automatic glass doors and stops when she's about six inches from the doors. She backs up and tries again, but nothing happens. She turns and looks at me in confusion. I look at her, equally confused and stand up and jump on the sensor mat. Still nothing. Adrian looks at me in wide-eyed panic.

"I can't let them find me out here. I'm in the hospital for *cancer*!"

"Just say you were getting some fresh air," I tell her.

"You mean tell them I was wandering the streets with their $10,000 piece of medical equipment?"

"No, just –"

"*Get me in!*"

I look at her, confused.

"Go! Run!" she motions towards the other side of the building.

I throw down my cigarette in defeat and I run. Around the back of the building, around the side of the building, and to the front, where I make sure to stop running well before anyone in the lobby sees me. Once I'm past the lobby I walk as quickly as possible, down the hallway, turn, down another hallway, and turn again. I'm completely lost. I back track and try another hallway, but it's no use. I can't find the disappearing door. I'm just about to give up and go back outside and around again, but I decide to try one last corridor. At the end I see our door. I run down the empty hallway and through the sliding doors, but Adrian's nowhere to be found.

"Addie?" I call tentatively. I can see our cigarette butts on the ground. I know this is the right door. I step out a little farther and watch Adrian drag her IV stand from around the corner, through the decorative stones and past some shrubs.

"What are you doing back there!"

But she doesn't answer. Instead her eyes open wide and her mouth drops open. I whip my head around and leap towards the glass doors as they slide closed again.

"Shit!" I scream, before taking off back around the building, through the lobby, and down the shiny linoleum hallways again.

***

The next day, tired of the 5th floor, I decide to explore. The doctors gave Adrian a shot of something or other through her IV that knocked her out. She's been sleeping soundly for the past couple hours and I'm growing restless. Leaving the familiar smell of our room I begin my trek about the hospital.

To the left I can hear an old woman arguing with her caregiver about the infamous standards of hospital cuisine. "But Mrs. Ferguson, you *have* to eat."

"You eat it," she rasps with the voice of a 40-year-smoker.

I turn right, and with no regard for social etiquette, I begin peering through the door of every room I pass. A couple doors down from Adrian's room is an elderly woman. I saw her the day we came. A younger woman, her daughter I assume, keeps vigil by her side. There's just enough time for me to watch the younger woman, one hand holding the patient's hand, reach up to caress the woman's hair with her free hand while gently leaning in to whisper something to her. They disappear from my vision, the moment's gone, and I continue on.

I pass a couple closed doors, turn left and wander down the

hallway. To my left is the chaos of the nurse's station and to my right another row of doors. Another old woman, and another, an old man and another old woman. From the last door echoes the sound of chimes. I glance in to find yet another elderly woman, alone and sickly with tubes running from every opening in her body. I pause for a moment, mouth open, gawking at the horror before me. Her frail body looks alien. Even from the distance of the door I can see the bulge of the needle under her sallow skin which has reached the point of near transparency. I can hear the rhythmic rise and fall of the respirator, her lungs inflating to the tune of the systematic beeping of her heart rate. I picture her in her youth with long flowing hair and sparkling eyes and fear washes over me. This will be me one day. But will I be alone? The alone part is what scares me the most. How sad to die alone. I want someone there for her, holding her hand, caressing her forehead as I saw moments before.

I turn another corner and before reaching the elevator, I catch a glimpse of yet another aging, dying man. I passed his room a number of times the day before and even earlier this morning. Not once have I seen anyone in there with him. He's in a main hallway with glass widows surrounding him; his loneliness on display for all to see. I hesitate and debate going in to talk to him. But what will I say? Will he be rude? What if he tells me to get the hell out? I picture wheeling the other lonely woman into his room so they can just drift off together...

"But what's the point?" I think to myself. *"We all die alone."* And suddenly, I feel completely alone.

The unnaturalness of Adrian's presence in this place hits me. There's a reason I feel out of place. It's because I shouldn't be here. Adrian shouldn't be here. I follow the blue stripe of carpet down the hallway and with each step the reality of our situation is hammered into me. Twenty-four-year-olds don't get cancer. But they do. Right or not, it happens and there's no stopping it.

A coldness that starts with my chest constricting to shallow breathing, makes its way down my spine and towards my fingertips. Panic. I'm going to die. Adrian's going to die. It doesn't matter what they do to save her now, it's prolonging the inevitable. So what's the point? Of any of it?

I step aboard the stark sterilized elevator and immediately turn forward. The shiny sheets of silver meet and I recognize the hazy image of my own reflection. My stomach leaps as my body begins to drop before abruptly coming to a stop on the fourth floor.

In step a man and woman with two young children.

"Hold on to the handrail Jimmy," the man says.

"For God's sakes Frank, it's an elevator, not a roller coaster," the woman snaps as we take off with a jolt.

The whole family stumbles as the elevator begins to drop. The whole family that is, except the man. He stands in the corner, as stable as can be, hand firmly clasping the rail, a smug, triumphant look on his face. We continue to drop to the lobby. The doors open and the family exits.

I decide to stay along for the ride to see where I end up.

The elevator rises again to the fifth floor and I'm back where I started. A man with five children enters, four boys ranging in age from seven to thirteen and the youngest, a girl with curly pigtails. The children's eyes are red and swollen and the little girl's breath comes in jagged gasps. From her little neck hangs an adult-sized crucifix. I look to the man's eyes and it's all too clear. They are minus a member. I ride with them to the bottom floor. I want out. I don't want to be witness to their grief, making a spectacle of their pain. As the elevator lurches to a stop I feel my stomach heave and fear I might lose the soggy ham and cheese hospital cafeteria sandwich I ate earlier. As they leave, the man reaches down and scoops the little girl up in his arms, clinging to her. It's not a protective move. It's desperation. Loss. He buries his face in her hair so that the sob escaping his mouth is barely audible and he hurries towards the glass doors, his four other children following him in a line like little ducks.

The elevator doors close again and I'm trapped with their lingering grief. I need to escape this death I feel penetrating through every pore in my body. I picture the sickness seeping in, clinging everywhere, impossible to escape. It's in all that I touch; from the sink handles to the old used sheets and fluid stained gowns. An awful taste lingers in my mouth. The sterile recycled air that I breathe mixes with the dead flesh from the ham sandwich. Death. It's everywhere, caught in the hairs of my nasal passage in a cocktail of bad breath and medication. Everywhere I turn I feel death and sickness pushing in from all sides. I need comfort. I need affirmation of life. I search the elevator directory. "Neonatal care unit, floor three." I push the button to the third floor.

The door once again slides open and the sight that greets me sends an immediate wave of peace throughout me. The third floor is the only floor that is easily distinguishable. The walls are lined with hundreds upon hundreds of tiles each with a tiny handprint of various colors and a name written beside each one.

"God, I hope this isn't a memorial wall," I think to myself.

I stop to read some of the names and noticed they're not all infant prints. In fact, some appear to be only a size smaller than my own. Most tiles contain a single handprint, but staggered throughout are tiles containing two little tiny handprints with similar names; names like Peter and Patricia, Mandy and Sandy, Billy and Bobby, Valarie and Malarie.

It must be the décor, but I feel myself revert back to the maturity of a child. "Dick. Who in this day and age names their child Dick? Elementary school is hard enough already, why put your child at a disadvantage? I can only hope it's a family name.

As I read the names, I begin taking inventory of the ones rhyming with any body part, function, or excretion. "Bart-fart, Luke-puke, Harry-Carrie, Virginia the vagina, Nichole the butt-hole," I sing to myself.

I should probably be on the psychiatric floor rather than the children's floor.

I wander past the labor and delivery room and into the waiting room. But no one is waiting.

I stop at the nurses' station.

"Excuse me, is there an infant viewing room?"

"Oh yes, it's right around the corner. Who are you here to see Hon?" asks a middle-aged Asian woman in her busy polka-a-dot uniform. She turns towards her computer, fingers poised, ready to call-up my information on cue.

"Oh, uh, no one," I tell her hesitantly. "I just want to see them. Is that alright?"

Her eyes soften as she tilts her head and smiles. "Of course you can dear. Just head straight down this hall and take a left. You can't miss it."

I take a couple wrong turns, I back track, and finally find it. But when I find it, I'm met with disappointment. Only three? In the movies it's packed. Reality can be so disappointing.

I lean my forehead on the glass and peer in. Two tiny little red wrinkled balls squirm in their caged beds. And the cutest of all, a little Asian baby with a blue knit cap, lays in silent stillness. I almost feel guilty, looking to these tiny helpless balls of newly formed life for comfort.

"Which one is yours?" asks a guy who will forever in my mind be known as Danny...

"Oh, none of them. I'm just looking." I tell him, quickly wiping my tears before turning to face him.

Beside him lays one of those little innocents wrapped tightly in a white blanket. He looks down at his daughter with eyes of hopes and dreams to come that only a father can possess.

I look down at her and my heart melts. She's perfect.

Beside Danny stands an older man with graying hair. His suit pants, maroon sweater-vest and brown leather jacket reek of money, right down to his shiny tasseled burgundy loafers. There's an awkwardness between them I can't quite place.

Danny continues to oogle at his daughter, occasionally looking to this man for reassurance. He offers the wheeled-bottomed bassinet to the man.

"I've seen quite enough," the man says curtly.

Danny's face drops in disappointment and I instantly hate the man.

"I'm leaving now. Tell Margie I'll talk to her later," he says before strolling away.

I look over at Danny with the eyes of a parent and perhaps understand why this man was so short with him. Danny's straight reddish-blond hair falls limply to his chin, and his pierced ear and goatee do nothing to inspire confidence in his reliability. And with his dark starched jeans, white T-shirt, industrial style jacket, and wallet-on-a-chain, he hardly seems like the-up-and-coming professional. But the wonder and amazement in his eyes is all the requirements I need. He will be a loving father.

"Is this your first?" I ask him, searching for a way to fill the silent void left in the wake of the other man's rudeness.

"Yes, yes she it," he replies in a wispy voice.

"How old are you?" I ask.

"Thirty-seven."

Whoa. A piece of the puzzle falls into place. Thirty-seven with long hair, a goatee, and the attire of a gas station attendant. No wonder Danny isn't good enough for this man's daughter. Watching Danny, I flash forward 25 years from now and realize that no man will be good enough for his little girl either.

Danny and I chat for a bit. He tells me how excited he is to take his daughter to Germany to visit his grandmother before she dies.

Death. Again.

I watch him standing there, face full of emotion as he stares down in wonderment at his new daughter, and I realize I've found what I was looking for. In this brief moment, within the love and overwhelming emotion in his face, I have found a sliver of peace.

I leave the maternity ward in a dull state of mind and emotion. Exhausted, I return to the elevator and the fifth floor. With the exception of the hallway of tiny handprints, room to room, floor to floor, they've all looked, smelled, and tasted the same. There was no difference in the starkness of the linoleum floor or the tackiness of the rainbow curtains hanging from the widows of each room. The only variable from floor to floor was the people in it.

Having seen the respirators breathing life back into other patients, I'm thankful for the lone IV extending from Adrian's right arm as I curl up in the chair next to her, ready to join her in sleep.

***

I awake the next morning with a cloud of dullness remaining from the previous day. But today I'm leaving. Whether or not Adrian's released, my plane ticket is scheduled and I have my own life to return to. Her mom will arrive this evening two hours before my departure and will pick-up with Adrian where I leave off.

I immediately go in search of the test results that had been promised to us the day before.

"Well, good news! We don't know what's wrong with you so you can go home now," our new nurse says with a smile.

"Seriously?"

"She's hydrated, we don't know what else to do, so you can go home," he says, way too cheerful.

"God I hate the hospital," Adrian says, launching herself back against her pillow in frustration while I immediately begin packing our stuff.

***

Before I leave, Adrian has one last stop for me. If I'm going to see anything in Tampa, Adrian is determined it be this.

When we pull into the cemetery I give her a look. "You're kidding, right?"

She's not.

Rain has deterred mourners so we have the entire place to ourselves. Adrian mentioned this cemetery weeks before. She described it as a place where she could find utter peace. She leads me over to her favorite tombstone, our sole reason for being there. Towering in the middle of the cemetery stands a white marble angel at least twice my height. Her wings wrap around her and her hair flows behind her. In her hands is a single flower she clasps to her chest, her face reaching towards Heaven. Beneath her in simple bold block letters is the word "RESIGNATION."

"If there is one thing I wish to do in life," Adrian tells me as we stand side-by-side looking up at this angel, "it would be to resign from it. It all seems so peaceful."

I can't believe how at peace she is with her own death. I'm still frantic about my life, let alone even attempting to deal with her death, and she's just ready to resign.

I wander towards the cliff overlooking the ocean and a big gray marble structure catches my eye. I walk closer and realize it's a perfectly smooth marble bench at the edge of the cliff facing the ocean. It sits on a little stage and on either side are two huge urns. It's beautiful. That is until I see what's written across it in writing similar to that of "RESIGNATION."

Written on the back of the bench directly in the middle is a single word in quotations: "WAITING."

The moment I read it I begin to cry as I suddenly flash forward to myself at 85 in goofy plastic out-of-date jewelry and some tacky little straw hat with a flower in it. My body hunches over, my gnarled hands clasp my purse and my cheeks sag and cave with age. I see myself sitting, staring out at the ocean, completely and utterly alone. My husband is long since dead and my children are busy with their own children and their own lives. I imagine myself playing cards to pass the days and sitting on the bench talking to my husband as if he's still by my side. I see tears slide down my old withered face and realize I'm grieving the loss of a friend; a companion. Not a lover. I can still feel his love as I imagine him there beside me. I feel it in the breeze and in the last bit of warmth from the sunset kissing my face. It's his response that I miss, not his touch.

Suddenly I'm so incredibly scared of my own future. But it's not death that I'm afraid of, it's the thought of sitting here, looking out over this cliff, spending my last precious days of life "WAITING" to die.

I walk back towards Adrian who's still standing in front of her angel, face turned upwards while the rain continues to fall. I grab her hand and look up towards the angel, squinting as the rain hits my own face. I glance sideways and realize she's not shrinking from the rain in the least. I turn my head back up towards the angel and let go of the instinct to shield myself from the downpour. I take in the shock of the cold patter hitting my forehead and my cheeks, contrasting with the warmth of my tears. I breathe in the salt of the ocean and the clean smell of rain mixed with fresh cut grass. I watch as drops of rain, trapped in the grooves of the carving, follow the feathers on the angel's wings, cascading down towards the word, "RESIGNATION". In that moment of release, I feel like maybe I've caught a glimpse of what it means to Adrian to resign from it all. The words from her book come back to me with new clarity:

> *"If there were any way of sheltering from death's blows –*
> *I am not the man to recoil from it…*
> *A man who has learned how to die has unlearned how to be a*
> *slave."*

Tendering My Resignation

Acknowledgments

First and foremost thank you to the Creator of all creativity and to the Bestower of all blessings. I have been truly blessed.

To my loving, faithful and unwaveringly supportive husband. Thank you will never be enough.

To my weekly WAGGERS: this would never have been possible without you. Thank you for your insight, your encouragement and for keeping my brain from turning into mommy mush. Your guidance and critique have made this a better book and me a better writer and your friendship has made me a better person.

To Cindy, Pamela, Tom and Brad: thank you for keeping the houses still standing while we chase those crazy dreams of ours.

ABOUT THE AUTHOR

Jessica Lincoln is an award-winning young adult author. She has been addicted to writing since eighth grade, but never considered writing for a career until she was in college. After earning her journalism degree, she realized she would much rather write about the people in her head than the people on the street, so she quit her job and began writing full time and hasn't looked back since.

She lives in Washington with her husband, two kids and a puppy named Bella. She loves volunteering and celebrating life.

You can connect with Jessica on Instagram, Facebook or her website; www.JessicaLincoln.com

www.ingramcontent.com/pod-product-compliance
Lightning Source LLC
Chambersburg PA
CBHW021122020426
42331CB00004B/583